ROMAN TIMES

Dragon Books
Granada Publishing
8 Grafton Street, London W1X 3LA

Published by Dragon Books 1984

Copyright © Hachette 1978
This edition copyright © Granada Publishing 1984
British Library Cataloguing in Publication Data
Miquel, Pierre
   Roman times. – (Everyday lives)
   1. Rome – Social life and customs – Juvenile
   literature
   I. Title   II. Au temps des romains. *English*
   937   DG78

ISBN 0-583-30678-0

Printed and bound in Spain by
Graficas Reunidas, Madrid

EVERYDAY LIVES

ROMAN TIMES

By Pierre Miquel
Illustrated by Yvon Le Gall

DRAGON BOOKS
Granada Publishing

CONTENTS

THE STORY OF ROME

The story of Rome began in a small farmers' settlement built on seven hills in Latium in central Italy. According to ancient tradition, it was founded in 753 B.C. A succession of kings, Roman and Etruscan, turned what was a collection of oval thatched huts into the walled city of Tarquin the Proud. In 509 B.C. the Romans threw Tarquin out, and created the Republic which, within 500 years, had become the only power in the Mediterranean world. First Rome conquered Italy, then Spain, Greece, the Near East, Gaul (France and Belgium), north Africa and Egypt; also the islands of Sicily, Sardinia, Corsica, Crete, the Aegean islands, Cyprus and Rhodes and finally Britain. The Empire was complete – but, as the saying goes, it was not built in a day.

The Republic

The Republic was ruled by elected magistrates, called consuls, the Senate and the voting people of Rome. A citizen army defended the city, and made Rome's first conquests. The legionaries who fought Hannibal and the Carthaginians in the Punic Wars (third and second centuries B.C.) were not mercenaries but conscripts, and a hundred years later Julius Caesar's army in Gaul and Britain, apart from some paid foreign auxiliaries, was still manned by Roman citizens. These soldiers, peasant farmers when they were at home, had always had to work hard on the land, planting wheat and tending their olive trees like all the other farmers of the ancient world.

Unlike the Phoenicians, Carthaginians and Greeks, the Romans remained homebound until one overseas conquest after another completely changed their lives. Prisoners of war brought home by the legionaries were sold and resold, put to work on the land, in the mines, or as servants in the mansions of the rich. These slaves relieved the more fortunate from toiling on the land, carrying arms, digging wells.

But slaves must be fed. How do you look after a whole family of slaves on a small plot of land? You can't. So the better off bought the small farms at rock bottom prices. Little by little, every inch of fertile land in Italy was covered by enormous estates instead of small farms. The peasants left for Rome or the big cities. There they joined the masses of poor citizens – the plebeians (*plebs*) – living on handouts from the rich *patricians* and eventually from the State itself.

FIGHTING MEN OF THE ROMAN ARMY

There were 300,000 infantrymen in the 50 legions of the Roman army. All were citizens.

From Augustus's time there were 4 squadrons of cavalry (120 men) serving with each legion.

In addition there were non-citizen auxiliary troops. They were often cavalry, archers or slingsmen. Each cohort of auxiliaries had from 500 to 1000 men enrolled in centuries.

The Empire

Had Julius Caesar (101–44 B.C.) not been murdered, he would have ended the Republic by becoming the first Emperor. This role fell instead to his adopted son and successor, Octavian (63 B.C.–14 A.D.), who was called Augustus. He alone, like the commanders-in-chief of old, now held absolute power (*imperium*).

During the first two centuries A.D., the Empire reached its greatest extent. *Britannia* (Britain) was conquered together with *Frisia* (today's Holland), the Rhineland, the northern Alps, the lands of the Danube including Romania (*Dacia*) and all of Asia Minor. The Roman frontiers were extended in this period beyond Syria and Judea into the Arabian desert, and in the end Rome ruled the whole of the known western world.

The legionaries knew nothing of the Americas across the Atlantic Ocean. That is why they gave Cape Finisterre in Spain its name, *finis terrarum*, meaning the end of the world. They did, however, know that there was more to Africa further south, across the Sahara, but did not want to cross a desert as broad as an ocean. They also knew that there were vast territories, peopled by nomadic tribes who spoke germanic languages, to the north and east but the Romans decided it was not worth conquering them. They just made sure these 'barbarians' did not cross the frontier.

The map on pages 12 and 13 shows the extent of the Roman Empire.

WONDERS OF THE ROMAN WORLD

You could visit five of the wonders of the world
– all within the Roman Empire:

* ★ the mausoleum of Halicarnassus in Asia Minor

* ★ the pyramids of Egypt

* ★ the statue of Zeus at Olympia

* ★ the temple of Artemis at Ephesus

* ★ Pharos, the great lighthouse of Alexandria

ROMAN TOWNS IN BRITAIN

Verulamium	St Albans
Ratae	Leicester
Deva	Chester
Isca Dumnoniorum	Exeter
Londinium	London
Dubris	Dover
Mamucium	Manchester
Eboracum	York
Danum	Doncaster
Lindum	Lincoln
Aquae Sulis	Bath

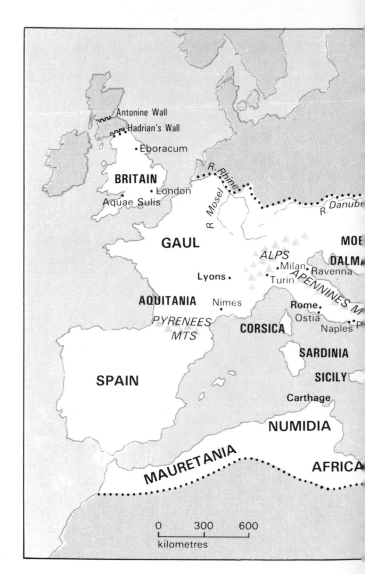

Antonine Wall
Hadrian's Wall
• Eboracum
BRITAIN
• London
Aquae Sulis
R. Rhine
R. Mosel
R. Danube
GAUL
ALPS
MOE
DALM
• Milan
• Ravenna
APENNINES M
Lyons •
• Turin
AQUITANIA
Nimes
Rome •
• Ostia
PYRENEES
MTS
CORSICA
Naples • P
SPAIN
SARDINIA
SICILY
Carthage
NUMIDIA
MAURETANIA
AFRICA

0   300   600
kilometres

12

THE ROMAN EMPIRE

DACIA

BLACK SEA

ASIA MINOR

Byzantium

MACEDONIA

AEGEAN SEA

PHOENICIA

GREECE

CYPRUS

JUDEA

Athens

RHODES

CRETE

MEDITERRANEAN
SEA

Alexandria

RED
SEA

EGYPT

R. Nile

•••••• Borders of the Roman Empire

13

The State Religion

In this closed world, heir to all the riches of Antiquity, the Roman Empire gave its head of state unlimited power. From the time of Augustus, no person or institution could compete with the emperor's might. He was head of the army and first magistrate of the city; he controlled the administration of state affairs and the dispensation of justice. He was honoured as a god. In every province there were temples dedicated to 'Rome and Augustus' where incense was offered up at the altar of the emperor.

The Romans imposed some of their gods on the peoples they conquered, but they were also quite willing to adopt foreign gods. Only the Jewish people and later, in their footsteps, the Christians opposed this policy. Theirs was a fierce resistance because they worshipped one god, totally rejecting all others – including the emperor. It took several military campaigns to defeat Judea, which revolted twice.

Pax Romana

From her immense Empire, Rome drew enormous riches which led to great prosperity. A unified system of money, weights and measures together with the *Pax Romana* – a state of peace throughout the Empire – encouraged the free circulation of goods. And the capital cities, towns and great ports were important markets in themselves.

With a population in the second century A.D. of 1,200,000, Rome became the most important commercial centre in the whole world. Tunisia and Egypt sent great shipments of wheat to the city. Vast warehouses stored corn, oil, wine, salt and every kind of food and drink. Luxuries poured in from everywhere. Industrialists and mineworkers looked for tin in Britain or gold in Dacia, exploited Spanish mines or worked the ore beds of the Aegean islands.

Little by little, the Empire united all the cultures surrounding the Mediterranean. Everywhere people led similar lives. The inhabitants of any city would be accustomed to Gallic pottery, Syrian fabrics and Greek wines. Arms were imported from Spain, hunting dogs from Britain and iron ploughs from Gaul. Citizens of the Empire dressed similarly everywhere and women followed the same styles. Fashions set in Rome were copied from Alexandria in Egypt to the shores of the Black Sea.

Spreading the Word

The Roman Empire's ability to assimilate foreign
countries and cultures owed much to the spread of
the Latin language, but most of all to her amazing
technological feats. Some 90,000 kilometres of roads
traversed the Empire. Traffic was heavy, though the
fastest vehicle could travel only 45 kilometres in a
day. The roads were straight and safe, with regular
milestones and roadhouses. They were an essential
feature of Roman control, enabling troops to be
redeployed rapidly to any troubled area.

Nonetheless most important traffic went by sea. In
the well-run ports, often equipped with lighthouses,
slow boats with triangular Latin (lateen) sails or
square Greek ones were loaded with corn and pots
(*amphorae*) of oil. The return journey to Egypt from
Rome might take ten weeks; it took courage for a
Roman to cross even the English Channel in those
days. But in time the Romans learned not to be scared
of the sea. They sailed for pleasure and to take part in
the festivals organized by the great cities of the
Empire in imitation of Rome.

In Gaul, races and gladiatorial games were organized in the great amphitheatres of Nimes and Arles
as well as Byzantium and Africa. Roman theatre was
not confined to Rome but was performed in the
towns of Gaul, Africa and Spain. A busy trade in wild

beasts from Africa made circus games possible even on the Rhine. The Romans exported along with Latin, mortar and chariot races, their bloodthirsty taste for brutal entertainments.

Nothing, to outward appearances, distinguished a Roman town in Africa from one in Gaul. The civilizations of the Mediterranean, thanks to Rome, were cast in a single mould. This common culture influenced every part of everyday life in the western world, and in many places it still does so today.

KEY DATES IN ROMAN HISTORY

THE LITTLE KINGDOM
550 B.C. Foundation of Rome
509 B.C. Rome becomes a republic

THE REPUBLIC
The Republic is established and Rome gra-
dually extends her power in Italy and overseas.
300–218 B.C. Rome conquers Italy
    73–71 B.C. The great slave revolt of Spar-
                 tacus
         44 B.C. Julius Caesar, conqueror of Gaul
               and invader of Britain is assas-
               sinated.

THE EARLY EMPIRE

Rome dominates the Mediterranean and western world.

23 B.C. Octavian takes the title of Augustus and becomes emperor.

A.D. 54–68 The reign of Nero

98–180 The 'Golden Age'

212 All male citizens of the empire become citizens of Rome.

THE LATE EMPIRE

The gradual decline of Rome

258 First of the great German invasions

410 Rome is taken by Alaric I, King of the Visigoths.

476 End of the Roman Empire in the West.

This book describes everyday life mainly in the last century of the Republic and the first two centuries of the Empire.

ARMY LIFE

ACTIVE SERVICE

The soldiers of Rome were infantrymen, called legionaries because they were grouped in legions. Each legion was a combat unit of 6000 men divided into 10 cohorts of 600 each. In each cohort there were three maniples, tactical units of 200 men. Finally these were divided into two centuries. Centurions, the lowest ranking officers, were so named because they commanded 100 men.

Senior officers had once been elected by their men, but under the Empire the emperor appointed them. These military tribunes, especially the legate of the legion, were directly responsible to Rome. Legions in barracks on frontier guard duty were commanded by officers called camp prefects.

The 20th Legion enrols new recruits. Each recruit's family name is inscribed on a register while he is given a medical check-up. In the early Republic those who avoided conscription could be sold as slaves.

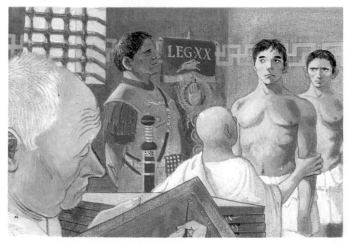

On a forced march the soldiers carried all their equipment
for eating, sleeping and fighting. They often travelled up to
50 kilometres a day on foot.

23

In their barracks the legionaries wore yellow overalls and leather helmets. This was their uniform for daily chores: looking after the animals, cleaning their quarters, or military exercises.

Each legionary was entitled to four bushels of corn a month (roughly 900 grammes a day) which was kept for him in special military warehouses. When these were empty the legionaries requisitioned corn – or even harvested it

themselves.

At first the legionaries were all conscripts in compulsory military service. Every Roman male between 17 and 60 could be called up and was expected to pay for his own equipment and arms. Soon, however, the state began to pay the soldiers. In Imperial times Rome had to maintain a standing army of 300,000 men. They were well paid, especially by Augustus, and when they retired were given 3000 silver denarii or a small farm of their own. Rome's conscripts had become a professional army.

The legionaries were well looked after. They were housed, fed and clothed and there were baths and hospitals to care for them. In exchange they swore

Veterans, old legionaries who have done fifteen or twenty years' service, are rewarded by the emperor with medals, money or land. Many soldiers dreamed of the day they could retire to their own farm.

allegiance to their general and submitted to the army's harsh discipline. Military crimes could be punished with floggings or death.

The legionaries also had to work hard. As raw recruits they learned drill and handling arms. Then there were manoeuvres in open country sleeping in tents, forced day and night marches, or learning to swim or jump in full armour. They also had to be navvies, lumberjacks, carpenters, bridge-builders and masons. They built their own camps and fortresses and most Roman roads were originally made by the legionaries. Sometimes they drummed up local labourers to do heavy work, and then they would be quite happy to stand back and supervise them!

THE GREATEST ARMY IN THE WORLD

The legions maintained a permanent guard over the frontiers of the Empire, which extended to the ends of the known world. The Romans ruled the shores of the Mediterranean, most of the Near and Middle East, north Africa up to the desert, Europe as far as the Rhine and Danube and Britain up to Scotland. Relatively few legions were needed to keep order: the whole of Egypt, for example, was controlled by only two legions – a mere 12,000 men.

'Throw the crow!' yelled the captain of a Roman galley who wanted to board the enemy. The 'crow' was a hinged gangway, eight metres long, with a long spike at the end which stuck into the enemy's boat enabling the soldiers to charge across.

Grouped around their standards and led by their centurions, the legionaries charged forward, sheltering behind their great shields. After throwing their javelins they started hand-to-hand fighting. The Romans' swords were shorter than the barbarians' ones but their helmets and breastplates protected them, and they fought in disciplined groups.

Soldiers raiding a barbarian village (right) set fire to the huts and killed the able-bodied men. Women and children were led away as slaves. All property of any value was gathered together and the soldiers shared it out.

In northern Europe great walls held back the barbarian tribes, with ditches and guard towers. In Britain, Hadrian's wall (built in 123 A.D.) stretched from the Solway Firth to the mouth of the Tyne. The Romans also employed large numbers of barbarians as soldiers or auxiliaries, mostly as cavalry or lightly 28 armed footsoldiers.

Legions were grouped into armies for campaigns. To punish the revolts of Numidian tribes or incursions by Germans across the Rhine, the emperor would send a general with two or three legions. By forced marches along the straight Roman roads (where they always had right of way) the soldiers were soon at their base camp. Then they would advance into enemy country behind their scouts, each night building a fortified camp.

Battles also followed a regular pattern: cavalry on the wings, infantry in the centre. The men grouped themselves behind their standard, which they would defend to the death. On the defensive they formed

Prisoners of war, like these Germans (above) captured near the Rhine, were humiliated by the Romans. They forced the leaders to march to Rome in chains, with ropes around their necks, to feature in the general's triumphal procession (right).

three lines, and protected one another with their shields. When they attacked they charged in lines, hurling their javelins and then fighting with their swords.

If he won, the general was awarded a 'triumph': Caesar, when he vanquished Vercingetorix the Gaul, marched in triumphal procession through the streets of Rome from the Field of Mars to the Capitol. Musicians played whilst the senators and magistrates of Rome walked behind the victorious general in his chariot. He was crowned with laurel and before him went the captive enemy leaders.

From Augustus's time, only the emperor was allowed to celebrate a triumph in this way.

WAR MACHINES

The Romans waged war scientifically. They adapted for military purposes the skills of the engineers, architects and technicians. As soon as a country was subjugated they began to build permanent roads of stone and to bridge the rivers. As a result, reinforcements could be brought rapidly from one part of the Empire to another. The Romans had inherited sophisticated techniques of siege warfare from the Greeks, which they developed further. Enemy towns or fortresses were encircled by ditches bristling with spikes, as well as forts and camps.

Then enormous catapults and other siege machines were brought up. With these they threw stones

An assault tower closes in on the barbarians' stronghold.

**The sappers have knocked down the ramparts. The legion
moves forward in 'tortoise' formation, shield to shield,
almost invulnerable behind a wall of iron.**

against the walls, flaming missiles against wooden
gateways or arrows against men. Battering rams
enabled them to attack the walls whilst sheltering
from enemy missiles.

The most successful engine of war was a high
wooden tower on wheels. They pushed it slowly
against the walls. Then they lowered a drawbridge
and soldiers poured out over the top. The tower itself
was protected from fire-arrows by a covering of fresh
animal hides.

**The ballista (right) was a giant crossbow used for setting fire
to wooden ramparts or thatched roofs. The arrows carried**
burning rags soaked in pitch.

At this point the Rhine is 400 metres wide, but the Roman army has to cross. With great stone pile-drivers they drive heavy beams into the riverbed to make fifty columns, which they join together with girders. In a few days the legions cross on a wooden bridge four metres wide.

Pull! The massive oak ram, hanging from a beam, smashed
the gates of a town. Behind it men pull with ropes and then
release it suddenly. After smashing into the gates the ram
swings back into position for the next attack. A roof of
stretched skins protects the legionaries operating it.

Although the Romans' technological resources
prevented their besieged enemy from making sorties,
they could not always breach the walls if they were
solidly built, so sieges could be long. Sometimes they
had to wait until the enemy, driven desperate by
hunger, tried to escape.

The Romans built their war machines on the battlefield. The
catapult on the left is a sort of giant spoon powered by a
heavy counterweight. It could throw a missile weighing
eighty kilograms for up to 500 or even 1000 metres. The arm
of the onager ('wild ass') on the right is stretched by a
windlass.

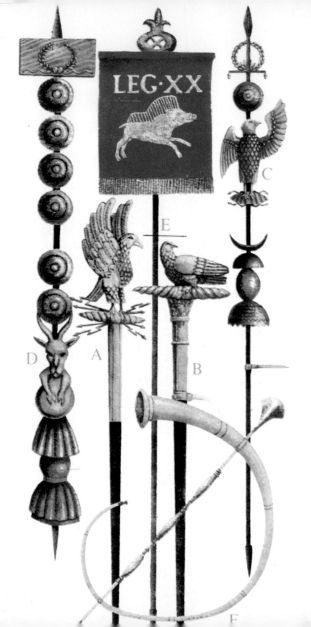

LEG·XX

D   A   E   B   C

F

RAISING STANDARDS

By following his standard every soldier knew where he should be in even the most confusing of battles. The eagles were the insignia of the whole legion (A and B). C is the insignia of a corps of auxiliaries. The insignia of the maniples usually consisted of crowns and animals (D). The cavalry flag was called a vexillum (E). The trumpeter was responsible for directing the legion's movements by his notes. F is a horn of the legions of Trajan.

Helmets
The helmet of a Roman legionary hardly changed over the centuries. It was a metal skull-cap with a flat rim all round. This was narrow at the front but widened back from his ears to protect the neck. There were also large neck guards. Officers' helmets could be mounted with colourful plumes.

The helmets shown overleaf are, from left to right: (1) Helmet of Tiberius's legions (first century A.D.), (2) Helmet of the XX Legion in Nero's time, (3) Helmet from the early second century A.D., (4) Helmet of a legionary of the first half of the first century A.D.

Swords
Swords varied in length. Over the centuries they grew from 50 to 84 centimetres. The swords pictured on page 41 in their scabbards all date from the first century A.D. (5,6,7,8). The little dagger in its scabbard on page 42 (9) is from the same period.

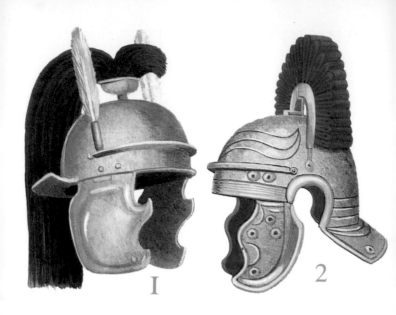

Javelins

Javelins measured between 2 and 2.1 metres, on a shaft 7 centimetres thick and 1.4 metres long. The one on the left (10) dates from the second half of the first century A.D., the central one (11) from the end of the second century and the one on the right (12) from the early second century A.D.

Shields

Shields were oval or rectangular. The heavy rectangular shield (13) belonged to a legionary of Trajan's time. The oval one (14), which was lighter, dates from Tiberius's time. The sling (15), used by slingsmen from Majorca or Minorca, hurled deadly balls of lead (16).

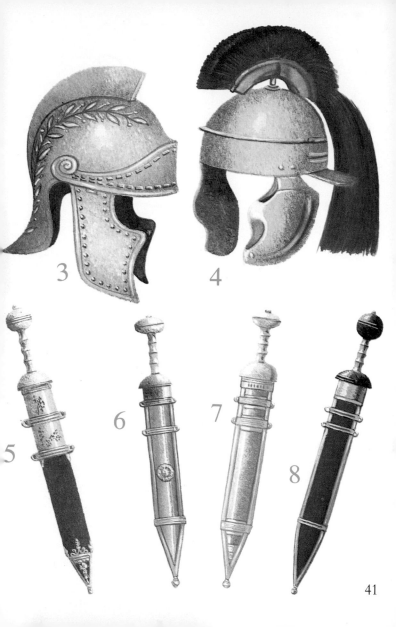

3

4

5

6

7

8

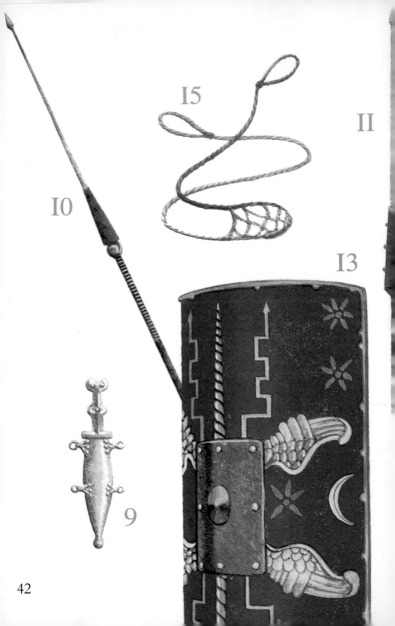

15

11

10

13

9

16

12

14

A LIFE OF TOIL

A steward allots tasks to slaves on a great estate.

Although the Romans knew how to make butter, they did
not eat it; they preferred olive oil. Enormous amounts were
produced commercially. In this country press they are
46 extracting the oil from ripe olives.

Gaul, North Africa, Sicily and Egypt were the
wheat-growing areas of the Empire. The Treviri, a people
living on the banks of the Mosel, invented the first reaping
machine. Iron teeth pulled off the ears of wheat, rye or oats
which fell into a wooden box.

LIVING OFF THE LAND

'Do you walk on your hands?' exclaimed a rich
Roman to a peasant who showed him his calloused
palms. Under the Empire, Roman citizens, rich and
poor, never ventured into the countryside even
though their ancestors had been farmers. They
despised the work and life of the land. As a result
Rome had to import almost everything she needed to
eat and drink.

And why bother to grow it yourself, when Egyp-
tian corn cost less than Italian in Rome's markets?
Why bother working when the emperor fed the plebs
for doing nothing? Fortunately for the Romans, the
great estates of north Africa and Gaul produced rich
crops of every kind.

These huge agricultural estates belonged to
immensely rich families, who used skilled slaves to
cultivate them. There were vineyard workers, 47

shepherds, herdsmen and labourers, and the work was directed by a steward called a procurator. When the ready supply of slaves diminished after the end of the great wars of conquest, many of these estates had to be broken up. Sometimes they were leased to free farmers or freed slaves (freedmen), who would rent the land for a payment in kind or money.

Summers were hot and winters quite mild in the Mediterranean climate, and they could grow vines and olives as well as corn. On the larger estates, some farmers already used nitrate fertilizers. The biggest profits came from breeding small animals such as sheep or goats near to the cities, or horses on stud farms further away. Nonetheless farm work usually required a large work force for a relatively poor yield. Forty-seven workers were needed for 100 hectares, and only rich owners could maintain a workforce large enough to develop their estates. Though in some areas we hear of estates with three or four thousand slaves!

By and large the Romans only drank the milk of sheep and goats. To improve milk yield they grew laburnum bushes in their fields. Cows were only to be seen in the damp lands of Britain, Gaul and northern Spain.

Grapes were crushed by barefoot men dancing to the flute.
The finest wines came from Greece, Cyprus, Syria and
Falernus in south Italy. The latter was kept for twenty years
before drinking. There were vineyards in Britain too.

The Roman plough was made entirely of wood. It consisted
of three pieces. The supple shaft was made of laurel, the
beam which held the ploughshare was of green oak and the
ploughshare was a hook of oak, bronze or iron.

Great profits were made at Ostia and elsewhere from the salt pans, which were owned by the State but operated by private individuals. Salt was used far more than nowadays especially to season and preserve fish and meat.

WORKING IN INDUSTRY

The mines of Rome were prisons where first slaves and then condemned men were sent – especially Christians. Working conditions were hellish. Men collapsed in their hundreds in the humid galleries, or under the torrid sun in the open-cast quarries.

The Romans searched far and wide for minerals. Expeditions were sent to Britain, long before the legions, to search for tin. Caesar probably came to get control of the mines. Gaul, rich in iron, was coveted until she was finally conquered. The Emperor Trajan made war on the Dacians, today's Romanians, to take possession of their gold mines. The very early conquest of Spain is explained by the importance of her resources, which included lead, copper, tin, iron and mercury mines!

Generally the mines were underground. Access was by shafts, far less deep than today's but very badly lit and ventilated. Galleries where convicts 50 worked were very rarely supported by props. The roofs were low – barely a metre high – so the miners worked kneeling or lying down.

Tools were rudimentary: a hammer for breaking rocks, a pick, a shovel, wedges. The ore had to be transported on men's backs in baskets, and then hauled to the surface by block and tackle.

The gold mine at Dolocauthi in Wales was drained by a huge wooden water wheel whilst aqueducts up to seven miles long brought water to wash the ore.

Work was no less hard in the stone quarries. Rock was cut in steps. The blocks were hewn roughly into shape where they stood, and then lifted out. Powerful cranes hoisted them on to boats or carts which transported them to building sites. Transport was in fact more expensive and time-consuming than the mining itself.

Wool was first boiled in water and pork fat, then beaten, sorted by hand and carded with a comb with curved teeth. It was woven in government workshops.

An open cast stone quarry. 53

These men grimacing with effort are working in a lead mine in Spain. Oil lamps light a gallery which, most unusually, is supported by wooden props. Fatal accidents and illness decimated these slaves who breathed in the toxic fumes of oxidized lead.

The Romans used two kinds of tiles together – flat and semicircular. They are still used in the south of France. In the trench a worker is mixing the clay. The tiles are shaped in moulds and dried in the open air, then baked in the furnace.

In marble and limestone quarries they detached the enormous blocks of stone needed for the construction of temples or public monuments by driving wooden wedges into chiselled holes. When these were soaked in water they swelled, splitting the rock.

BRICKS AND MORTAR

The Romans were the finest masons of the western world. They built unbelievably solid monuments, some of which still stand, for they were not only masons, but also architects, engineers and surveyors.

The Romans used rubble and a form of cement to make their concrete. The result was very different from ours, but no less strong. To build a wall, for instance, they first of all surrounded the foundation area with boards; then they poured in a bed of mortar, and piled pebbles and rubble into it. Then the wall itself was built up with alternating layers of mortar and quarry stone or brick. Afterwards it was coated with reddish cement or decorated with frescos painted on stucco, with bas-reliefs or rich facings of marble.

The builders mostly used brick but would also try any available local stone – the soft volcanic tufa from the hills of Rome, or the travertine rock (a hard, yellowish form of limestone from the Tiber region) used to build the Colosseum. To move stone blocks and fit them closely into place they used cranes powered by men in treadmills.

Roman houses, built of brick and timber, must have looked remarkably like Tudor half-timbered houses. Shaped stone was reserved for great public monuments such as the 13 aqueducts which supplied Rome with drinking water. The Romans built such structures in the vicinity of most large towns. The

An aqueduct under construction.

Workers tile a building with a technique still in use today.
The flat tiles are placed in the gaps and the round ones cover
the beams.

famous aqueduct in Gaul now known as the Pont du
Gard can still be seen. Its three tiers of arches reach a
height of 48 metres; the highest tier is 273 metres long
and it carried 20,000 cubic metres of water daily to
Nimes. The water from the aqueducts was distributed in the towns by a system of very broad lead
pipes. The plumbing in the city of Lyon, up to 20
centimetres in diameter, totalled 26 kilometres in
length and weighed 2000 tonnes!

This enormous crane is unloading blocks of stone for a
temple. Men walking in treadmills turn winches that lift the
blocks via a system of ropes and pulleys.

The Romans used every available stone quarry. They needed materials for building roads, aqueducts, public buildings and temples. They often brought marble from very far away for their temples.

The legionaries were constantly reinforcing the town's fortifications. Here (top right) they are raising a wall of dressed stone. The blocks are joined by iron clamps and sealed with lead.

The Romans knew how to build huge domes. During construction (right) they supported them with huge wooden moulds. The Pantheon in Rome is still standing with its roof intact.

TRADES AND CRAFTS

Some of the finest blacksmiths of the Empire were in Britain and Gaul. For generations they had used charcoal to smelt the iron ore in their rustic furnaces which were fanned with bellows. Iron was used everywhere and in many different ways.

It was used by coopers for rings encircling barrels, as well as for making swords, and two-wheeled ploughs with metal ploughshares. These ploughs were superior to Roman ones as they could work heavy, damp soil. The Roman plough only had a wooden 'snout'.

The soil itself was raw material for the potters. There were skilled native potters in Britain and elsewhere before the Romans came, but they were soon having to compete with vast pottery factories set up by the Romans. Pottery was very important in everyday life, and most household items were made of it: oil lamps, vases, dishes or statuettes. Amphorae were used to transport oil and wine.

There were a hundred and one other trades in any city: small shopkeepers, wine or beer sellers, silk traders, drapers, dyers, workers in ivory, goldsmiths and shoemakers. All of their goods had to be transported about Rome on men's backs. An army of porters, dockers and street traders created an unending hubbub in the narrow streets of the city. By law

A blacksmith at work.

In this pottery workshop (above), the potters first work fresh, damp clay roughly by hand, then the bowl is shaped by the turner before going into the oven. Vases were usually decorated before firing. The design was worked on to the piece which was then fired and glazed.

drovers could only drive their carts through the city at night, and many people complained of the noise they made keeping them awake. By day teams of mules, rich men's carriages and the great mass of people, busy or idle, created frequent traffic jams in the alleys and lanes. And many people in the crowd were particularly busy – picking pockets!

This baker (right), installed in front of his oven, sells luxury wheat bread with aniseed and cummin seeds. The poor mostly ate barley or millet bread.

The wine quays stretched along the Tiber near the Aventine Hill. There two or three thousand amphorae of wine were warehoused – imports from all over the Mediterranean. Most of these wine merchants also ran taverns like this (right). Women were forbidden by law to drink there.

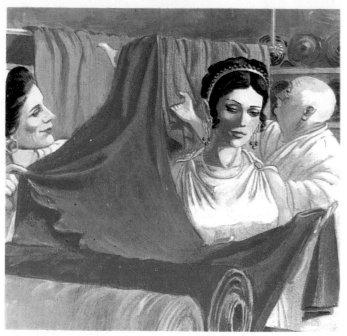

The Romans generally wore woollen clothes bought at the drapers. They could be fine or coarse, plain or brightly coloured. These women (above) are buying the more expensive linen cloths. It was already possible to buy silks from the Far East, if you could afford the price.

The legionary (right) is chatting while the cobbler nails new leather soles to his shoes. They wore out quickly on the rough stone roads. The Romans could make cavalry boots and all sorts of sandals, but many of them still went barefoot.

ART TO ORDER

The Romans were very fond of bas-relief sculptures.
Their artists learned the technique from the Greeks,
and adapted it to create vivid portrayals of scenes
from everyday life. They worked to order, and there
was never any shortage of customers.

Most of their work was commissioned by the
emperor and his thousands of officials. They wanted
their military victories pictured on columns or triumphal arches; Trajan's column, for instance, told the
story of his campaigns against the Dacians. Artists
were expected to represent things as accurately as
possible. They showed legionaries clutching ladders
thrown over town walls, warships, charging cavalry
and chained prisoners of war.

Statues were commissioned by individuals. A
blacksmith of York ordered a sculpture of himself at
work; some Tiber sailors had their boat depicted
transporting corn; a family man commissioned a
carved tombstone for himself, showing him together
with his wife. Thousands of such sculptures were
made throughout the Empire.

Painters were not as much in demand as sculptors
but one fashion kept them busy. They decorated the
walls of rich houses with vast frescos representing
mythological scenes, geometric designs, still lifes and
so on, or they painted the plaster to look like marble.

The workshop of a bas-relief sculptor.

The Romans made marvellous mosaics. The artist created a sketch for his work, then marked it out in squares. On each square he placed small cubes of stone or glass. The cubes were stuck together with a special glue made of resin, gum or pitch.

The floors of such houses would also be covered in splendid mosaics.

Roman artists had many specialities. They were masters at carving cameo figures in relief on layered stones. They produced very high quality tableware (a silver service of 102 pieces was found down a well in Pompeii in 1894), and knew how to make fine glassware and beautiful ceramics. The Romans inherited from the Greeks a taste for refinement in the objects of everyday life.

The painter's assistant has used a pestle and mortar to grind the pigments which the artist is mixing on his palette.

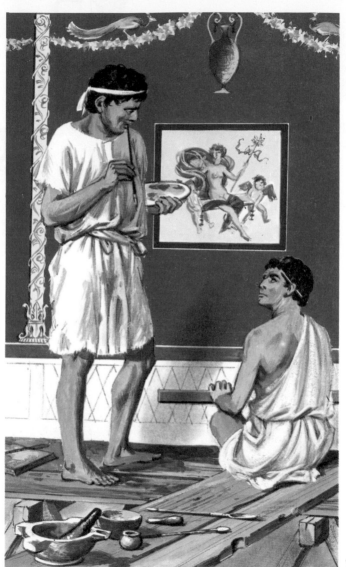

The Romans excelled in the minor arts which add pleasure to everyday life. Here you can see a cameo (1), a fine glass carafe (2), a ring (3), a golden bracelet (4), a chased silver goblet (5) and a bronze lamp (6).

We know all the emperors of Rome from their busts (right). Hundreds of statues of them were erected throughout the Empire so that all its inhabitants would know their ruler. Other rich and powerful Romans, particularly the senators, were also sculpted.

4

5

6

LIFE IN THE CITY

Architects had an almost impossible task in trying to house 1,200,000 inhabitants on the seven hills of the old city of Rome. The absence of rapid means of transport forced them to build in the city centre – only the very poor resigned themselves to living outside the walls. The plebs crowded together in unhealthy homes in the slum quarters.

Within the walls, people could only build upwards. The wealthy few could afford their palaces and private mansions with gardens, fishponds, cool courtyards and arcaded walkways. The poorer majority lived in *insulae*, blocks of flats which looked much like modern ones. They were built in squares around inner courts. Augustus limited their legal height to 20 metres, but the need to accommodate people was more pressing than the law, and veritable skyscrapers grew up like the block of flats known as *Felicles*, which became a real tourist attraction.

The 45,000 flats in Rome boasted few comforts. They were heated by charcoal braziers and water had to be fetched from a ground floor fountain. Houses were often built on steep hillsides, which could lead to amusing incidents. One day a bull rushed into a ground floor flat on one side, and fell out of a third floor window on the other!

Rome had 85 kilometres of streets and alleyways. Only the main roads which crossed the city (such as

74   **A traffic jam in a busy street.**

the Sacred Way, Ostian Way and Latin Way) were paved, clean and well maintained. The alleys were dirty, muddy and dimly lit; people emptied all their rubbish (even their chamber pots) into the street. Where pavements existed, they were crowded with stalls and peddlers.

In these conditions, fire was a constant threat. Firemen made slow progress and there was seldom enough water to put out a major fire when they arrived. In the reign of Antoninus Pius 340 houses were burnt in a single day. In the great fire of 64 A.D., when Nero was said to have fiddled while Rome burned, thousands of Romans died.

Rome had multi-storey buildings but the water from the aqueducts came only to the ground floor. Water carriers served the tenants, though the young folk still liked to come to the fountain for a small amphora of water . . . and a chat.

Rome's markets had much the same produce as a southern
European market today, except that there were no potatoes
or tomatoes. The stalls offered fresh or dried fruit and
vegetables as well as fresh and salted fish and meat.

The Colosseum took its name from a giant gilt bronze statue, fifty metres high, which the Romans called the Colossus (left). Officially it depicted the Sun God, but it looked remarkably like Nero who had it built. The Colosseum was also known as the Flavian Amphitheatre.

In the taverns the Romans drank and played at dice, and discussed politics or the day's news. Work stopped well before sunset so Rome was full of idlers. Tavern keepers diluted the wine with water.

Fire terrified the Romans. Arsonists were punished by burning at the stake and anyone who caused a fire by accident was publicly beaten. Rome had firemen and even primitive fire engines; here a chain of inhabitants (left) conveys buckets of water.

OVER THE THRESHOLD

The man was absolute master of the Roman house-hold. Marriages were arranged by the head of the household or *paterfamilias*, often the grandfather. The wedding ritual was most important. The bride entered her new home for the first time accompanied by her new husband's friends. The best man would go first, carrying a nuptial torch of hawthorn, then the others carried the young woman (who might even be as young as twelve) over the threshold – without letting her feet touch the ground. White linen cloths were draped around the walls, and the columns were decorated with laurel leaves and ivy leaves, symbols of strength and health. At least three bridesmaids followed the bride, one carrying a distaff, another a spindle. It was the duty of the third,

Each home had its family altar dedicated to the household gods (the Lares), represented by statuettes. Worship was conducted by the head of the house, the father, while the rest of the family recited prayers and made offerings.

In the heart of the Roman house the *atrium* was lit by an opening in the roof, the *impluvium*, through which rainwater could also be collected. In summer the sun was kept out with a curtain. The atrium was the centre of family life.

The bride is carried across the threshold of her new home. 83

In front of the whole family the *tonsor* (barber) cuts a young man's first beard, carefully gathering up the hairs. There was no set age for this ceremony: it had to wait until the young man had a beard!

the maid of honour, to lead the bride to her nuptial bed.

During all this time the bridegroom had to wait outside the door with the wedding guests. Then, after throwing nuts to the children, he could come in, go up to his wife, and symbolically offer her water and fire.

In the early Republic the father, as head of the household, had the power of life and death over his children. He could refuse to recognize them, or sell them as slaves. But, little by little, the law began to protect children and their mothers against excesses of an all-powerful father.

As for the women, some eventually claimed equality very unsubtly. They competed, dressed as men, in chariot races. They practised swordfighting or wrestling although they were officially forbidden to appear in the amphitheatre. But Rome also had its learned women: lawyers, politicians, writers. If her husband disapproved, a woman could in certain cases divorce him and ask her parents to take her back home. If her husband repudiated her, she had the right to reclaim her dowry.

Children were cared for, when they were very young, by their mother or a wet-nurse but they were quickly put in the hands of slaves, freedmen or teachers – that is, in rich families. Children from poor families taught themselves the wisdom of the streets.

This man has just died. He is positioned on a funeral couch as though he were still alive. Behind him a nurse and professional mourners weep. Branches of fir on the front door warn passers-by that there has been a death in the house.

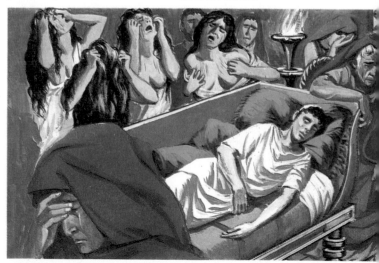

BREAD AND BANQUETS

Most people in the cities had a poor diet of cereals and starchy foods – bread and porridge – and cheese, with little in the way of green vegetables or fresh meat. Breakfast was usually a glass of water with some garlic bread, and lunch was rarely more than a cold snack. Supper was the Romans' main meal. Everyone, especially the rich gluttons, took great pains over the big meal at the end of the day when the family came together, often inviting their friends.

In summer the feasting usually finished at nightfall, but it sometimes lasted all night. Table companions

The baker heats his oven with wooden faggots, and his slaves turn heavy stone mills to grind the flour. Bakers bought grain in government stores, baked this, and sold it back to the stores for free distribution.

Ordinary people mostly ate coarse bread, broad beans, chickpeas, cabbage soup and bacon. They had to filter and water down the wine before drinking it. The whole family ate out of the same plate which was kept warm by a sort of brazier.

A rich man's kitchen, where an army of slaves prepare never-ending banquets on charcoal braziers.

lay on couches around a low table, propped up on their left elbows. They used spoons to serve themselves, knives to cut the bread, and toothpicks, but they used their fingers rather than forks for eating.

The guests drank honeyed wine at the beginning of these meals and ate small, hot bread rolls with every dish. Their wine was decanted from *amphorae* into bowls, then diluted with water. Servants filled the guests' glasses by dipping them into the bowls. There could be seven courses or more on the menu. After the hors-d'oeuvre came three entrées, two roasts and the pudding. The entrées were substantial: poultry, kidneys, sows' udders (a dish the Romans were passionately fond of), hares or fish. The roasts might be young wild boar or veal, probably cooked with olive oil, and served with rich sauces.

Most well-to-do people's suppers were modest by comparison, and changed little. The meal would start with olives, tunny fish or anchovies, followed by a main course of roast kid or grilled chops and finished off with a pudding.

The midday meal (*prandium*) remained frugal even amongst the rich. Cheese, fruits and bread dipped in wine were enough to satisfy them till supper, when they would have a hot meal.

The Romans took their evening meal lying down, not seated. These banquets had many courses, and could last late into the night. Diners ate with their fingers, and some say they cleaned their hands in their slaves' long hair.

FROM ABC TO ORATORY

Roman schoolmasters were poor, badly paid and barely educated, and they had too many pupils. They often had to work as copyists at night. Their pupils, aged seven to fifteen, boys, girls and even slaves, learned to read, write and count. The school buildings, often unsuitable and open to the clatter of the street, could become icy cold in winter. Sometimes classes even took place beside the road or in other open places. And in primary schools corporal punishment was common.

The Romans did not worry much about educating the inhabitants of their conquered provinces, so long as the rich and important sent their children to special schools to learn Latin and Greek. The children of the wealthy everywhere learned to read from private tutors. Then they set off for one of the larger towns in their province to join select classes in grammar and rhetoric. They were taught chiefly by men from Athens, Pergamum, Rhodes or Alexandria, where there was a long tradition of education. In their early teens, the pupils were taught Greek and Latin literature, history, geography, music, mythology and mathematics. Then their education was rounded off with rhetoric classes, which consisted in the main of making speeches and writing letters in good Latin. It was above all the sons of senators, the future officials of the imperial administration, who needed to learn the rhetoricians' skills.

Although the Romans were excellent engineers, architects and technicians, they never established a

Children were beaten when they made mistakes in school.

Children played at knucklebones like adults but the latter
were more interested in the bets! Boys and girls rolled hoops
and knew innumerable ball games. The balls might be
apples or nuts, or pieces of leather sewn together and stuffed
with bran. They also played a kind of hockey. Children of
the rich had rarer playthings, including musical
instruments, toys and trained animals.

proper system of scientific or technical education.
Knowledge was passed on within the family, or a boy
might be apprenticed to a surveyor in the same way
as he was apprenticed to a stonemason. Only profes-
sions which led to administrative careers were
officially taught, because the rich were only
interested in them.

The teacher of oratory (right) was called a rhetor. His
students had to be able to make speeches in Latin and Greek
and they usually also learnt the speeches of the great Roman
orators by heart. To become an aedile or a senator in later
life one had to be able to speak in public.

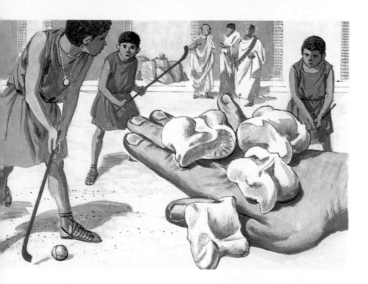

95

Great families entrusted their children to tutors. Herod Atticus, a rich Athenian, asked his son's teacher to parade in front of him large wooden boards on which were painted the letters of the alphabet. The child copied them on to a wax tablet using a metal stylus. He is also said to have had bread shaped like the letters, and an ivory alphabet.

Publishing was a laborious task in ancient Rome. Slave copyists (right) wrote out manuscripts by hand. One man read out the text, and up to ten others wrote it down. They used no punctuation, spaces between words or capital letters to clarify the text, and often made mistakes.

HEALTH AND HYGIENE

The Romans were meticulous about hygiene and cleanliness; simply taking a bath involved a ritual. First, they had a steam bath, then a hot water bath, then a cold water bath and finally a massage. Public baths were built by the state or the city council. Entry was either free or very cheap and great crowds of people went every day. Men and women were supposed to bathe at separate times.

Rome alone had several hundred baths, and Diocletian's baths covered an area of 13 hectares. Around the baths were arcades, stadiums for football, handball and gymnastics – and even libraries!

One of the ministries at Rome was responsible for water and the maintenance of the aqueducts. There were magistrates known as *aediles*, who had a special

Roman chemists generally used plants to make medicine. More than 500 species were used, most frequently hellebore, vervain, foxglove and lime. Sometimes something exotic was called for, like snake's venom or boiled stag's liver!

The Romans had public lavatories. At Dougga in Tunisia a lavatory has been found that could seat up to twenty-six people. Water ran continuously in a channel under the seats, flushing the excrement down a sewer.

responsibility for the sewers; one of them, named Agrippa, had the entire sewerage system of Rome cleaned at his own expense.

The citizens were just as careful about their health. They went for thermal cures to hot springs or made the fortunes of innumerable quacks who offered miracle cures and pretended to be specialists in treating this or that sickness. 'The only difference between the brigands and the doctors of Rome', said the great doctor Galen, 'is that the brigands kill people outside the city walls.'

Nevertheless there were many good doctors, notably Galen's own disciples. Roman surgeons could perform remarkably delicate operations including mending fractures, amputations, fitting artificial limbs, caesarian births, the extraction of kidney stones and trepanning (opening up the skull). The real doctors charged fees that were beyond the means of the poor country people, who consulted local wise women or used traditional cures instead.

99

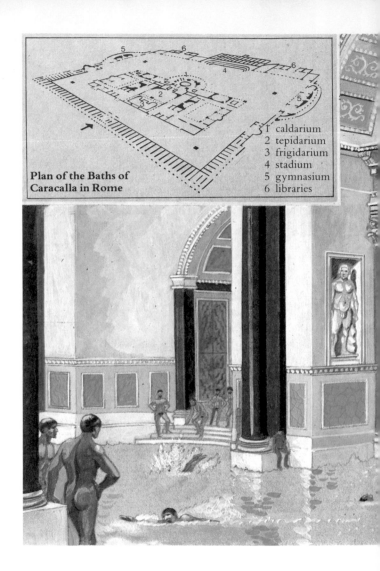

Plan of the Baths of
Caracalla in Rome

1 caldarium
2 tepidarium
3 frigidarium
4 stadium
5 gymnasium
6 libraries

The Roman baths: the *frigidarium* (cold bath). In the
background you can see people – and steam – emerging from
the warm and hot bath rooms (*tepidarium, caldarium*). 101

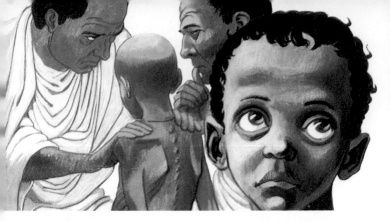

Children were often the innocent victims of epidemic illnesses like typhus, but also of malnutrition. Travelling doctors, usually slaves or freedmen, saw patients at fairs and markets.

The barber often acted as doctor or even surgeon. He could make poultices and plasters to heal wounds. Here he has shaved a patient's skull, then spread one of his pastes on to the wound with a spatula and a balsam spoon.

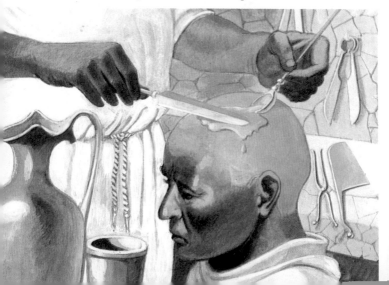

This Roman woman has just given birth seated in a chair. She is being given her baby by the midwife. Midwives were not formally trained. In difficult cases a doctor could be called.

Some medical and surgical instruments: (1) speculum, (2) pincers, (3) enema syringe, (4) cupping-glass, (5) scalpels, (6) hook for separating the edges of a wound, (7) lancet for pricking blisters, (8) forceps for extracting teeth, (9) clamp, (10) forceps, (11) saw, (12) lever for raising a broken bone.

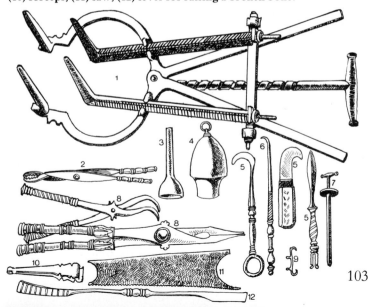

A ROMAN – FROM HEAD TO FOOT!

Originally a simple small cloak, the toga was made bigger and bigger until it reached a diameter of 6 metres. You needed someone's help to put it on. For ritual sacrifices the toga was worn right over the head.

The Romans had no underwear as we know it – no pants, socks, vests, and bras. The only undergarment worn by either sex was the tunic, which reached to below the knees for men, below the ankles for women. In the days of the Republic, men wore only a loin-cloth under their toga.

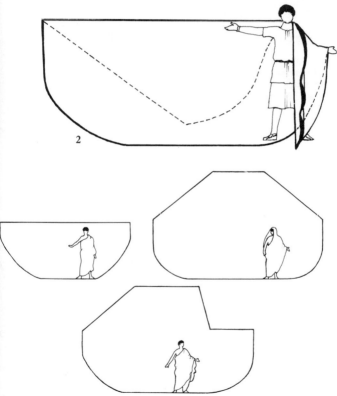

The top is folded back (1) and one end is placed over the shoulder and left arm (2). Then the other end is wrapped around the front of the body, over the left shoulder (3) and back to the right hip (4). Other variations on the style were possible!

Making up a rich Roman matron took a long time. Her slave expertly dresses her hair, keeping the curling irons hot on a brazier. Curls were kept in place with pins. White hairs were pulled out till a wig had to be worn.

The toga, which seems originally to have been Etruscan, was the only garment of the ancient Romans. Magistrates' and boys' togas were bordered with a band of purple. This robe, called the *praetexta*, was worn by youths until they were sixteen when they took on the *toga virila*, which was all white.

Under the Empire togas were worn less and less, and then only for special ceremonies or in the Senate. Over the tunic, people came to wear instead a light cloak, the *pallium*. The tunic itself became the outer garment worn over an inner tunic or *camisia*, which might have long sleeves attached. With foreign influences Romans took up narrow trousers, breeches, a thick hooded rain cloak (*paenula*), or the *caracalla* (another kind of cloak).

Women also wore long tunics under a narrow cut gown, the *stola*. They wore a cloak called the *palla* to go out. Romans seldom wore hats; women carried a fan shaped like an ace of spades, and sometimes a 106 parasol.

Women's hairstyles were often very complicated, and varied from one period to another. When a woman's hair was not long enough she would wear a wig. Till the middle of the first century styles were fairly simple (D). The honeycomb or diadem (C from front, B in profile) first appeared under the Flavians. At her wedding a young girl would gather up her hair in plaits on top of her head (A).

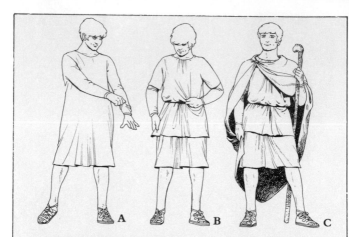

Over the long-sleeved tunic (A) a shorter, short-sleeved one was worn (B). A cloak pinned together over the right shoulder with a brooch completed the outfit (C).

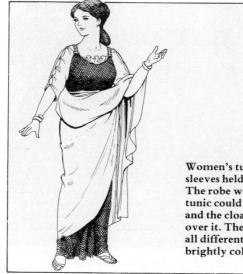

Women's tunics often had sleeves held by brooches. The robe worn over the tunic could be sleeveless and the cloak is draped over it. These clothes were all differently, often brightly coloured.

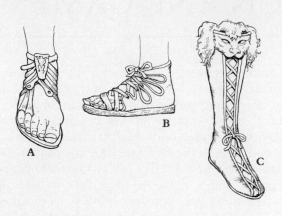

More or less open laced sandals were the commonest
footwear (A,B). Closed shoes which came up to the ankle
were made from fine leather. Philosophers and
simple-living folk contented themselves with light sandals,
often made of papyrus (D). Peasants wore a rustic shoe (E)
laced across the foot. Half-boots (C) were supposed to be
worn only by certain divinities and the emperor as a divine
symbol. Some men did wear them, but they were regarded
as either insolent or soft.

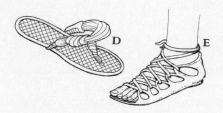

FUN AND GAMES

For his entertainment the man in the street went to the amphitheatre, or the hippodrome. A slightly more discerning public frequented the theatres. There were 250,000 seats in the Great Circus for chariot races; there were only 60,000 theatre seats in all Rome. But it is worth remembering that the largest theatre in the world today seats only 5000 people.

Roman stages were immense, not at all suited to intimate domestic dramas. Shows were grandiose with elaborate sets, and actors who were operatic tenors, mimes or comedians. They sang, danced or recited poetry accompanied by lyres and flutes. Thus the theatre transformed itself into a popular mass spectacle where the play was less and less important. It was singers and acrobats who were most in demand.

Early plays were performed in the street. Even after the city built proper theatres, there was a great deal of entertainment in public. Under the porticos strolling musicians gave concerts, while gamblers played with dice and dibs (knuckle-bones). In the evenings, people went off to the taverns. The big towns had a busy night-life.

Dance, fine music, the recital of poetry and reading of plays were the distractions of a small but rich élite. They took place in the private palaces of the rich. The

110   **Plays drew huge audiences to the theatres.**

The actor chooses his mask. In the Roman theatre the audience knew the character by the mask he wore. Any actor could play in quick succession a young girl, a dotard and a slave. The masks were of cloth covered in painted plaster.

artists were well looked after by their patrons and often lived in their houses. The virtuosi of the lyre or harp, who were in great demand, lived like princes and commanded fabulous fees. The Emperor Vespasian once paid 200,000 sesterces for a single performance on the cithara.

Strolling players livened up the city streets. They were not allowed to play the trumpet or the horn, because these were reserved for military and religious use, but they could use metal cymbals, double flutes, tambourines or pan pipes.

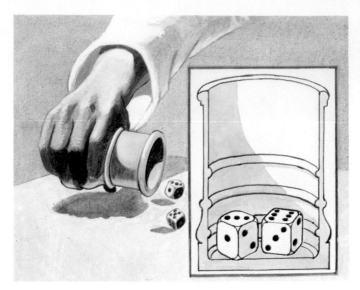

Watch out for cheats! Dice boxes had round ledges inside to force the dice to spin before they came out. It was thus supposed to be impossible to throw prepared numbers. Huge sums of money were played on dice especially by soldiers.

The rich (right top) gave concerts in their palaces. The lyre in the foreground has a sounding board of tortoise shell; in the centre is a hydraulic organ invented about 2,200 years ago. Water, moved by a pump, pushes air through the pipes.

Theatre seats (right) were hired or reserved but sometimes the crowd overflowed putting everyone out of place. So the owner has to restore order. His slaves throw out the interlopers.

115

BLOOD-LUST IN THE ARENA

'Caesar! Those who are about to die salute you.' First Julius Caesar, then Augustus and his successors turned gladiatorial combats into a kind of public institution. Laws obliged other cities to organize such fights and throughout the Empire arenas were built in the style of Rome's Colosseum which held up to 50,000 spectators.

In the provinces, the town councils employed professional consultants to run their games. They bought gladiators in the slave market or recruited ruffians and down-and-outs, subjecting them to a cruel training in special gladiatorial schools. In Rome the emperor's officials organized the show. His

Here are the gladiators. From left to right: a *retiarius* with trident, dagger and the net with which he entraps his opponent; a helmeted Thracian; a murmillo with Gallic shield, and a Samnite with a great Roman shield.

fighters, recruited from men already condemned to death, prisoners of war or adventurers, were housed in barracks.

The show opened with animal fights. The wild animals, like the gladiators, were brought in from all over the world. Here a rhino attacked an elephant, there bears set upon buffalos; soon the sand was soaked with blood. Then the wild animals were pitched against men – a dangerous sport but not always fatal to the humans. On some days more than 5000 carcasses were dragged from the arena.

The highlight of the show was provided by the gladiators. Like mock soldiers they marched, with their servants, past the emperor's box. On the great festivals there might be 1000, 4000, even 10,000 such

The angry bull gores the elephant in the stomach. He is tied to a giant ring so he cannot escape the elephant's charges which are directed by the mahout. The public loved animal fights.

The emperor gives the thumbs-up sign, granting mercy to
the vanquished.

The *bestiarius* was a gladiator who fought against wild animals. This lioness, wounded with a sword thrust, savages her tormentor before dying. The bear menaces his adversary while a lion, maddened by the crowd's screams, leaps on to another gladiator.

Many persecuted Christians and others condemned to death were tied naked to stakes and handed over to the appetites of starved animals. The mob loved these scenes of violence and death at the circus games.

A gladiator's fans have come down into the arena to congratulate their idol. Furious, the steward comes charging up: no one should be in the arena without his permission.

men. Partners were chosen by lot, and the pitiless combats began. The public cheered and took bets on their favourites. When a man fell to the ground, the victor looked to the emperor for permission to give the *coup de grâce*. If he gave the thumbs-up sign, the wounded man was lucky. If the crowd howled for blood and the emperor signed thumbs-down, the loser was killed.

LAYING BETS AT THE CIRCUS

Bread and circuses – this was the emperor's recipe for keeping the Roman rabble happy. Every month he gave them a flour ration. Well fed, hundreds of thousands of idlers, always ready for a festival, spent their days watching the shows in the forum, the theatre, the amphitheatre and the hippodrome.

There were nearly 200 festival days per year, not including the purely local or rural ones. There were festivals in honour of the gods, of the emperors, and of victorious generals, as well as traditional ones such as the *Ludi florales* (April 28–May 3), a gay, flower-decked carnival in honour of Flora.

The most popular festivals were celebrated with circus games. A quarter of a million people would pack the terraces of the Circus Maximus to watch the chariot races. In a single day 100 races would be held, with teams driving seven laps of 1200 metres.

When the magistrate dropped a white cloth, the four horses of each *quadriga* were off, wildly cheered on by the spectators who had staked fortunes on them. Great clouds of dust were raised by the chariot wheels. At each end of the run the charioteers had to round the boundary stone without touching it. Accidents were common, sometimes fatal for the men, and for the highly valued horses.

The victorious charioteers became the idols of the whole city and could earn millions of sesterces. One,

A chariot race at the Circus of Caligula in Rome.

Aurelius Mollicius, had more than 100 wins before he was twenty. Some retired with 3000 wins. They were the lucky ones, since very few survived to profit from their exploits. Chariot races were far more dangerous than modern motor races.

When the races were over, the spectators were invited to the prize giving, where a huge banquet was given by the emperor.

Circus staff throw cold water on the smoking wheels (right). Chariots went so fast that the wheels could catch fire. The charioteer wore his team's colours and carried a knife in case he crashed and had to cut himself loose.

The Naumachia was a mock sea-fight in a specially flooded amphitheatre. The first was arranged by Caesar in the Field of Mars, flooded with water from the Tiber. The two thousand combatants were all prisoners of war or condemned men. Later, Augustus gave a Naumachia re-enacting the famous battle of Salamis at which the Greeks defeated the Persians in 480 B.C.

At the entrance to the Colosseum (right) the bookmakers shout their odds. People laid bets on gladiatorial fights as well as on chariot races. Money was placed according to the favoured chariot team's colours: greens against whites, or blues against reds.

A 'natural' landscape has been created in the amphitheatre. The trees are hung with gold; there are fountains of perfumed water. Then the wild animals are released and the hunters attack! They can shelter behind the turnstiles or in the round spiked baskets. The arenas are full to bursting. There are lions, bears, panthers, elephants and even crocodiles, all being tormented and killed by the gladiators. The day the Colosseum was inaugurated by Titus they killed 5000 beasts.

127

STATE, RELIGION AND EMPIRE

The men of the senate were not ordinary Romans. Those judged worthy to be senators were drawn from the patrician class – the richest citizens of the Empire. They played an important role in the state, sometimes attacking official policy, recommending war or peace, and approving or amending laws. And of course they did not always agree with one another. When they disagreed with a speaker, they signified their disapproval by covering their heads with a section of their togas.

But from Augustus's time, the emperor was definitely the master, even though he made a show of listening to the senate, and even though all his official proclamations bore the words: 'In the name of the Senate and people of Rome' (Senatus Populusque Romanus = SPQR). The senators did not even intervene in the nomination of the emperor, who often adopted his successor in his own lifetime. The legions might reject his choice and make their own – but no one ever asked the senate. The emperor could arbitrarily hire and fire the highest officials of state, and it was his appointees who drafted, proposed and executed regulations which had the force of law. The senate would only be consulted as a formality.

A session of the Senate under the Republic.

Citizens had to cross a mobile wooden footbridge in single
file to reach the voting urns. To vote they placed a wooden
tablet in the urn, marked either A (*antiquo*, I reject) or UR
(*uti rogas*, I accept).

Every Roman noble had his political clients, poor citizens with voting rights who acted as electoral agents for their patron and defended him under all circumstances. In exchange he paid them and gave them a basket of food each morning.

Being a Roman senator remained an honour, and was increasingly open to rich provincials, but it no longer had a real political role as it did in the days of the Republic. The magistrates of Rome, the consuls, tribunes, praetors, aediles, and quaestors, were still elected by the Senate – but the list of candidates was supplied by the emperor. The senators themselves were not elected but appointed from amongst members of the Senatorial Order which consisted of the richest citizens, those who possessed at least a million sesterces.

Full of honours and money, the senators shared the dignities and honorary magistracies among themselves. The emperor let them talk away, so long as they obeyed him in the end. Rome had forgotten the Republic. Since Caesar's time she had acquired the habit of following a dictator.

A magistrate brings the emperor's verdict to a condemned man. Behind the magistrate his assistants, the lictors, each carry an axe wrapped in a bundle of rods (fasces). The condemned were offered a choice: execution by the axe or suicide. Here the magistrate is offering a choice of suicides: by poison or the sword.

The magistrate of Rome addressed the people in the Forum from the *Rostrum*, so called because it was decorated at each end with ships' prows or *rostra*.

TALKING TO THE GODS

The trumpets sound, and the ceremony of purification begins. In front of the temple the priests are going to sacrifice a pig, a ram and a bull. The animals, decked out for the procession, are fat, gleaming, clean and adorned with ribbons and garlands. They circle the temple three times with the worshippers who wear wreaths of laurel on their heads. Then they are sacrificed. When the augur has finished examining the entrails of the victims, the best pieces are burned and offered to the gods on the altar, and the rest are distributed among the faithful or sold.

The instruments of worship and sacrifice were made in strictly traditional ways. An augur carried as his emblem a staff with a crozier, and a special knife to carve the sacrifice.

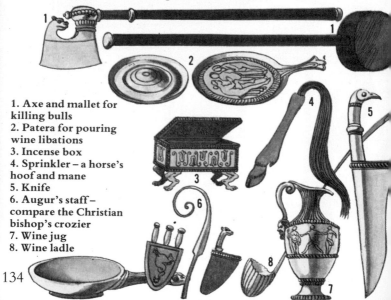

1. Axe and mallet for killing bulls
2. Patera for pouring wine libations
3. Incense box
4. Sprinkler – a horse's hoof and mane
5. Knife
6. Augur's staff – compare the Christian bishop's crozier
7. Wine jug
8. Wine ladle

Assistants (*victimarii*) present a bull's neck to the sacrificer, who raises the ritual axe. In his belt he carries a knife to dispatch the animal.

These animals are about to be ceremonially sacrificed.

The Romans believed in an eternal life but they needed the help of the gods to escape from this world. The state and its cities organized a minutely regulated worship of all the gods in their pantheon, especially Jupiter, Juno and Minerva. Wanting to have all available luck on their side, the Romans never hesitated to adopt foreign gods. In exchange they imposed their state cult on the countries they occupied.

The Romans' religion was full of rites and ceremonies. Priests organized continuous worship in

This man is an augur. The government has employed him to find the will of the gods. If the sacred chickens eat avidly, dropping scraps of food in their haste, he will declare that the gods favour the government's plans.

The bull's blood has been poured on the altar, and its belly
has been split open. The soothsayer (*haruspex*) is examining
the entrails, especially the liver.

their temples and sanctuaries, where they burnt vast
numbers of animals if the gods were angry. To avoid
angering the gods and to interpret the divine will, the
Romans followed the ancient practices of the Etrus-
cans. Some believed they saw signs in the sky, the
lightning or the stars, and in the entrails of sacrificial
victims. They interpreted ripples made by objects
thrown into water, or the way the wood burned in
the hearth. Yet others interpreted dreams. These
practices accompanied every public act, and formed
part of the rhythm of everyday life.

The Romans' fear of the gods affected the way they
talked in ordinary conversation. They swore by
Hercules, begged by Olympus or threatened by
Jupiter! If the gods appeared to be hostile to you, you
learned to respect destiny, and to submit serenely to
every ordeal, including death.

ROADS TO ROME

From the city of Rome to the furthest provinces, distances were measured in miles along the roads which the Romans built from the second century B.C. onwards.

A mile, one thousand Roman (double) paces, was about 1480 metres. The golden milestone of Rome, in the middle of the Forum, was the point from which all distances were measured. Stone markers were placed every mile throughout the Empire, from Britain to Syria, from the Danube to the Sahara!

The roads, made of crushed stones, were often narrow and badly paved. Only the famous imperial roads were straight and constantly looked after. They were wide enough to allow three carts to pass abreast

The Imperial Post used fast two-horse carriages. So did the rich who sometimes fitted them up to play dice, read and drink on long journeys. One emperor is said to have installed a revolving seat so as to see the countryside better!

Along the roads there were roadhouses for messengers and travellers which provided a resting place and fresh horses, repaired carriages and sold food. Some were built by the State, others by towns or private enterprise.

(slightly over four metres), and at the gates of Rome they could widen to 10 or 12 metres.

These roads were the vital arteries of the Empire. Without them the emperor's messengers could not travel fast and the legions could not rush, by forced marches, to a threatened province. In their way, they were works of art. In Italy there were tunnels a kilometre long, lit by torches. The Apennine Way crossed a valley 197 metres wide on a viaduct. 141

142

The Romans built about 90,000 kilometres of roads across the Empire.

A grand reception is laid on when a general and his legion come to town. The council comes out to welcome them and the population throw flowers to the soldiers as they march through the streets. Then comes a religious ceremony at the temple, and a banquet where a great many toasts are drunk to Rome and the emperor's health.

Sometimes the road was constructed on an embankment several metres high.

Roman roads were very robust. You began to build them by digging out two parallel ditches to drain off the water. The base of the future road was next cleared away to the bare rock and then recovered with sand and mortar. Four successive beds of stonework were piled up to a depth of 1.5 metres, and surfaced with flat hard stones. The surface had to be cambered to allow rainwater to drain away. These roads were built to last centuries, and some sections are still intact today, after two thousand years.

Silk is brought from China across the deserts of central Asia by camel caravans (below). This trade attracted the Romans to the Far East and brought fabulous riches to the merchants involved. Silks were greatly coveted by the rich.

TAKING SUPPLIES TO ROME

Some 1,200,000 Romans had to be fed every day, yet the Italian countryside was becoming less and less productive. It was a tough problem for the government. All the city's supplies came by sea and were unloaded at Ostia, the largest port in the Empire. Claudius and Trajan had two docks excavated at Ostia, covering more than 100 hectares. Two stone quays protected them and a lighthouse was built on an artificial island made by sinking a boat full of rocks.

The Romans built ports wherever their merchant fleet traded. Arles on the Rhone became the market-place for Gaul where wool, timber and wheat were collected for transport. In Egypt, Alexandria fulfilled the same function. Roman fleets also plied the Black Sea where they went to look for Scythian wheat and timber, and the North Sea where the traffic in wool and ore went through London. The principal commodities exported by Roman Britain were tin, skins, 146 pearls, sometimes grain – and slaves.

Egypt was the granary of the ancient world. Here you can see a scribe counting baskets of grain as they are carried on board by slaves. They will then be taken down river to Alexandria. Silks and spices and other products also came via Alexandria.

Merchants went up the Nile to acquire ivory tusks from black Africa. They fetched a good price in Rome. So did rhinoceros horns which were ground up and used as medicines.

Unloading timber in a Roman port.

149

Merchant vessels were made of pine, oak or cedar. The hulls were caulked with oakum, made from the fibres of old ropes and protected by tar, wax and paint. The nails used in shipbuilding were of bronze. The biggest boats, like the round and massive *Corbita*, were sail-powered; only light boats and warships were powered by oars.

Voyages were long and dangerous, and ship-owners who knew the risk they were taking insured their cargoes. When ships did arrive safely, however, the merchants could sell their cargoes for good profits to retailers or craftsmen. Huge warehouses (they covered six hectares at Ostia and even more at Rome) stocked all the produce of the ancient world: candles, torches, copy-books of parchment and rolls of papyrus, pepper and spices, wheat by the bushel, amphorae of wine, jars of oil, cloths and building materials – all that was needed for the life of the greatest city of the West. Without the ships' cargoes that came through Ostia, Rome would have died.

The Romans found barrels more suitable for transporting
goods by barge than their fragile amphorae. Sailors' guilds
used all navigable rivers for transport.

Accident! A cart full of empty amphorae has overturned on
the road. The team of bullocks panics. Journeys by road
were hazardous and slow, so river and sea travel were much
preferred. Most of the traffic on the famous Roman roads
was military.

ROMAN LIFE FOR ALL

Public land surveyors were always in the vanguard, building roads and public amenities, and designing new town layouts. Some countries conquered by Rome already had an urban civilization, but none had towns as large as Rome itself.

The Romans built temples, baths and theatres all around the Mediterranean. In north-west Europe they thoroughly Romanized the landscape: the former tribal capitals, ancient hill forts like Maiden Castle, had been little more than rough ramparts. In place of these the Romans built real towns with stone buildings, imposing gates, walls and beautiful houses.

The old chiefs deserted the countryside and their huge estates for the new towns and their fashionable

The centurion on the right (below) is checking up on his soldiers, vine stock in hand. He could strike a legionary for the least infringement of discipline. Sometimes the soldiers paid the centurion to avoid certain duties. This legionary, pilum in hand, guards the gateway of Trier in Germany.

Roman garrisons in Africa hunted wild beasts in the
hinterland. Lions that came down from the Atlas Mountains
to attack livestock on farms were systematically hunted down.

154

An engineer uses a surveying instrument to plan the route of an aqueduct.

way of life. The towns also became trading centres for the sale of the province's products, sometimes as exports to Rome.

From Augustus's time complete new towns were built for veterans of the legions at such places as Colchester in Britain, Turin in Italy and Autun in Gaul. Two or three thousand men with their families became the first inhabitants. They were given land, helped to build their houses and were provided with many of the essentials of town life such as drains and water.

Garrison towns, ancient cities, new towns or sea ports, the cities of the *Pax Romana* (Roman peace) all fostered a way of life that was above all Roman. The rich controlled the town councils, and paid the rural poor for casual labour when they needed it. The plebs of any city, gathered in the forum in the evenings, could be mistaken for the plebs of Rome: generally idle, hungry, gaily dressed and always eager for entertainment. Even in lesser towns like Silchester, the common workmen spoke Latin, and could read and write it.

Roman theatres were built in all the great cities of the
Empire in the open air. Enormous canopies were sometimes
stretched over them, usually by sailors, to protect the
audience from the sun.

It's a hard winter for the troops along Hadrian's Wall,
guarding the northern frontier of Roman Britain. The
soldiers live in wooden cabins in garrison towns. Still, they
are used to it. Most have not come from Italy, but from local
soldiers' families or from the local population, and
sometimes only the officers speak Latin. Merchants came to
the garrison towns, and the lands round about were
cultivated to supply food to the troops. Veterans settled
there when they retired, and so the temporary camp became
a town and the cabins were replaced by solid houses.

Index

159